Friendship Rocks

FRIENDS SHARE

by **Megan Borgert-Spaniol**

PEBBLE
a capstone imprint

Published by Pebble, an imprint of Capstone.
1710 Roe Crest Drive
North Mankato, Minnesota 56003
capstonepub.com

Library of Congress Cataloging-in-Publication Data
Names: Borgert-Spaniol, Megan, 1989- author.
Title: Friends share / Megan Borgert-Spaniol.
Description: North Mankato, Minnesota : Pebble, 2022. | Series: Friendship rocks | Includes bibliographical references and index. | Audience: Ages 5-8 | Audience: Grades K-1 | Summary: "Sharing can be tough. Sometimes we'd rather keep things, including our thoughts or feelings, to ourselves. But a good friend is generous with others. You can share your toys, your time, and so much more. Learn how to be a good friend by sharing!"— Provided by publisher.
Identifiers: LCCN 2021029716 (print) | LCCN 2021029717 (ebook) | ISBN 9781666315578 (hardcover) | ISBN 9781666320114 (paperback) | ISBN 9781666315639 (pdf) | ISBN 9781666315752 (kindle edition)
Subjects: LCSH: Sharing—Juvenile literature. | Social interaction in children—Juvenile literature. | Friendship—Juvenile literature.
Classification: LCC BF575.S48 B67 2022 (print) | LCC BF575.S48 (ebook) | DDC 177/.7—dc23
LC record available at https://lccn.loc.gov/2021029716
LC ebook record available at https://lccn.loc.gov/2021029717

Editorial and Design Credits
Editor: Jessica Rusick, Mighty Media; Designer: Aruna Rangarajan, Mighty Media

Image Credits
Shutterstock: anek.soowannaphoom, Cover, baibaz, 21, Darrin Henry, 11, Dmytro Zinkevych, 17, Friends Stock, 5, Monkey Business Images, 7, 16, Pixel-Shot, 15, spass, 8, Sudowoodo, 20, Syda Productions, 19, wavebreakmedia, 9, 13

Design Elements: Mighty Media, Inc.

All internet sites appearing in back matter were available and accurate when this book was sent to press.

Printed in the United States 5725

TABLE OF CONTENTS

Words in **bold** are in the glossary.

The Last Slice

You are at a birthday party. There is chocolate and vanilla cake. You want vanilla. But you see your friend take the last slice.

Your friend sees you are **upset**. She offers to share her slice with you. Sharing means giving part of something to someone else.

Equal Pieces

We can share in many ways. One way is by **dividing** something up. This means separating it into parts or pieces.

We divide things so there is enough for everyone. You and your friends are sharing pizza. What do you do? Cut it into **equal** slices!

Taking Turns

You can also share by taking turns. You and your friend both want to ride a bike. One of you waits while the other rides. Then you switch places.

You can share some things at the same time. You and your friend want to read the same book. Can you find a way to read it together?

Giving Time

People share things that can be held. These things include toys and food. People also share what can't be seen or held. One of these things is time.

Your friend doesn't understand his math homework. He asks you for help. You have homework too. But you give some time to help your friend.

Feelings

You can share feelings too. Your friend made you sad. You tell him why. This helps you feel better.

You can also share happy feelings. Your friend got a part in the school play. You share that you are happy for him!

Being Fair

We share to be **fair**. You and a friend go to the park. There is only one swing. You both want to use it. It's only fair to share! You take turns on the swing.

Working Together

Sharing helps people play and work together. A soccer team has to share the ball. If one person hogs it, the team won't do well.

You are working on a coloring **project** with a friend. Your friend forgot her colored pencils. You share yours with her. Now you can finish the project!

Feeling Good

Sharing isn't only about fairness or working together. Sometimes sharing just feels good. You baked cookies with your family. Your friend loves cookies. So, you bring her some. This makes her happy. You feel good that you made her happy!

Practice Sharing

A snack is a fun and easy thing to share with a friend. Practice fair sharing by following the steps below.

WHAT YOU DO:

1. Make a simple snack for you and a friend. You could spread peanut butter on slices of bread. Or, scoop yogurt into bowls and top it with fruit and granola.
2. Divide the snack into two bowls or onto two plates. Put an equal amount in each.

3. Let your friend choose the bowl or plate she wants.

Glossary

divide (dih-VIDE)—to separate into parts or groups

equal (EE-kwul)—the same as something else in size, number, or value

fair (FARE)—sticking to the rules, or not favoring one thing over another

project (PRO-jekt)—a school assignment that students work on over a period of time

upset (uhp-SEHT)—unhappy or angry

Read More

Bright, Rachel. *The Squirrels Who Squabbled.* New York: Scholastic Inc., 2019.

Cauchy, Véronique. *Line and Dot.* Washington, DC: Magination Press, 2018.

Ledyard, Stephanie Parsley. *Pie Is for Sharing.* New York: Roaring Brook Press, 2018.

Internet Sites

KidsHealth—Getting Along with Brothers and Sisters
kidshealth.org/en/kids/sibling-rivalry.html?WT.ac=ctg#cathome-family

KidsHealth—Group Projects for School
kidshealth.org/en/kids/group-projects.html?WT.ac=ctg#catschool

PBS Kids—Arthur: Arthur's Giving and Keeping Game
pbskids.org/arthur/friends/give-keep

Index

About the Author

Megan Borgert-Spaniol is an author and editor of children's media. When she isn't writing or reading, she enjoys doing yoga, eating croissants, and crafting homemade pizzas. Megan lives in Minneapolis, Minnesota, with a tall, goofy man and a small, chatty cat.